TELL ME WHY, TELL ME HOW

HOW DO PLANTS GROW?

MELISSA STEWART

 **Marshall Cavendish**
Benchmark
New York

Marshall Cavendish Benchmark
99 White Plains Road
Tarrytown, New York 10591-9001
www.marshallcavendish.us

All Web sites were available and accurate when this book was sent to press.

Editor: D. Sanders
Editorial Director: Michelle Bisson
Art Director: Anahid Hamparian
Series Designer: Alex Ferrari

Library of Congress Cataloging-in-Publication Data

Stewart, Melissa.
How do plants grow? / by Melissa Stewart.
p. cm. — (Tell me why, tell me how)
Summary: "An examination of the phenomena and scientific principles behind plant growth"—Provided by publisher.
Includes bibliographical references.
ISBN-13: 978-0-7614-2111-5 (alk. paper)
ISBN-10: 0-7614-2111-4 (alk. paper)
 1. Growth (Plants)—Juvenile literature. 2. Plants—Development—Juvenile literature. I. Title. II. Series.

QK731.S84 2006
571.8'2—dc22

2005017259

Photo research by Candlepants Incorporated

Cover photo: Lucido Studios Inc. /Corbis

The photographs in this book are used by permission and through the courtesy of: *Photo Researchers Inc.:* Laurie O'Keefe, 1, 23; Andrew Syred, 11; D. Roberts, 17; Stuart Wilson, 20. *Corbis:* Thom Lang, 4; Japack Company, 10; Michael Pole, 12; Frank Krahmer/zefa, 15; V. Brockhaus/zefa, 21; ER Productions, 24. *SuperStock:* age footstock, 5, 7, 9, 14, 16; Christophe Courteau, 6. *Phototake USA.com:* ISM, 13, 19; Dennis Kunkel, 22.

Printed in Malaysia
1 3 5 6 4 2

CONTENTS

Grass is one of the world's
most common plants.

Why Plants Grow

Go outside and take a look around. How many different kinds of plants do you see? Grass is a plant. So is a maple tree. Many other kinds of plants grow in parks, forests, backyards, and gardens.

Some plants manage to survive in the harshest places on Earth.

Scientists have found and named more than 260,000 **species,** or kinds, of plants on Earth. They also keep on discovering new species all the time. You can probably name some of the plants that grow near your home. Many other kinds of plants live in different parts of the world.

Like animals, plants come in many shapes and sizes. Think of the soft, spongy mosses living in a wetland. Now think of a giant redwood growing in an ancient forest. They look very different from each other, but they are both plants.

The duckweed floating on a pond lives for just a few months. Bristlecone pine trees can survive for more than 4,000 years. Some bamboo plants grow as much as 18 inches (46 centimeters) a day. A palm-like plant that lives in Mexico adds less than 1/2 inch (1 centimeter) a year.

The duckweed on a pond helps this frog stay hidden.

How many of these seeds do you think will grow into new plants?

All plants grow for the same reason. They need to make seeds that will grow into new plants. But how long a plant lives and how quickly it grows depend on what it needs to survive in its habitat.

In most places, bigger is better. Tall plants can soak up the most sunlight. Large plants are less likely to be eaten by hungry animals. Strong plants have the best chance of making it through fierce storms. But no matter what they look like, all plants have learned to survive on Earth.

Now I Know!

True or false: Grass is a kind of plant?

True.

7

You need food and water to grow and survive. Plants are no different.

What Plants Need to Grow

Think about some of the things you need to survive. Food, water, and a place to live are among the most important. Plants need these things, too.

You can buy food at the grocery store. You get water from a kitchen faucet or a drinking fountain. You live inside a house or an apartment that is kept at the right temperature year round. But for plants, getting what they need to live and grow is not always so easy.

These plants live in a warm, wet forest in Australia. It is the perfect place for them to spread and grow.

Most plants have three main parts: leaves, roots, and stems. Each of these parts plays an important role in keeping the plant alive.

A plant's leaves collect **energy** from the sun. The plant then uses that energy to make food. A plant's roots keep it

To live and grow, plants need energy from the sun.

firmly in the ground. Roots also **absorb,** or take in, water and **minerals** from the soil. The stem helps hold the plant up. It bears the plant's weight and keeps it from falling over. Special tubes in the stems of most plants carry water and minerals from the roots to the leaves. Another set of tubes moves food from the leaves to the rest of the plant.

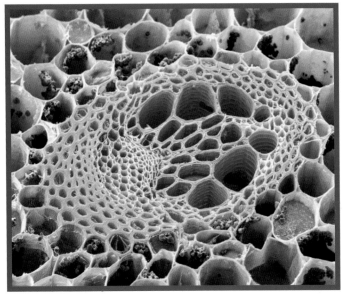

This photograph was taken through a microscope. It shows the tubes that carry water, minerals, and food from one part of a plant to another.

To survive, a plant needs enough space to spread its leaves and roots. It must live in a place that is not too hot or too cold. And it must get the right amount of rain and sunshine.

Now I Know!

What are the three main parts of a plant?

Leaves, roots, and stems.

A plant is held in place by its roots. This tree's root system is huge.

✹ Inside a Plant ✹

If you look through a microscope at a plant's roots, leaves, and stems, you will see that they are made of millions of tiny units called **cells.** Cells may be small, but they are very important. They control all the activities that keep a plant alive.

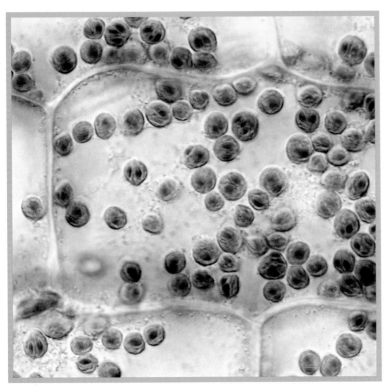

A cell is like a tiny house. A house has many different rooms, and each one has its own special role. You cook food in the kitchen, and you sleep in your bedroom. You would never try to park a car in the bathroom or take a shower in the garage.

This photograph shows what some of the cells that make up a leaf look like, when seen through a microscope.

Tiny organelles in the cells of these leaves collect energy from the sun.

Most cells have tiny parts called **organelles.** Each organelle has its own job to do. Some store food, water, and waste materials. Others control what materials enter and exit a cell. Special organelles in a plant's leaves collect energy from the sun. As long as a cell gets enough food and water, its organelles will keep working.

While a cell's organelles are hard at work, the entire cell is growing. When the cell reaches a certain size, it stops getting bigger and

splits into two separate cells. Then each of the new cells grows until it too is large enough to break in half. As the number of cells increases, the entire plant grows. Stems get taller. Roots become longer. More and more leaves appear. When the plant is old enough, it can reproduce, or create a new plant.

Now I Know!

Plants are made up of millions of
_____ ?

Cells.

This plant has just sprouted from a seed. It will continue to grow taller and spread out as its cells split to form even more cells.

Pine trees have small,
thin leaves called needles.

How Plants Make Food

A leaf's most important job is to collect sunlight, so a plant can make food. Different plants have different kinds of leaves.

This plant has large, broad leaves.

A maple tree's large, wide leaves can soak up a lot of sun during their short growing season. In autumn, the leaves fall off and flutter to the ground. Pine trees are different. They do not lose their leaves in autumn. Their short, thin leaves, called needles, keep collecting sun for most of the year.

Small plants sprout new leaves in early spring.

Trees get their leaves a few weeks later. This gives small plants time to collect lots of light before a tree's leaves block out the sun.

When the sun's sizzling rays strike a leaf, the light energy is captured by a green material called **chlorophyll.** Chlorophyll is found in special cell parts called **chloroplasts.** Most leaf cells contain about fifty chloroplasts.

Like most plants, the sunflower relies on the sun's light for its survival.

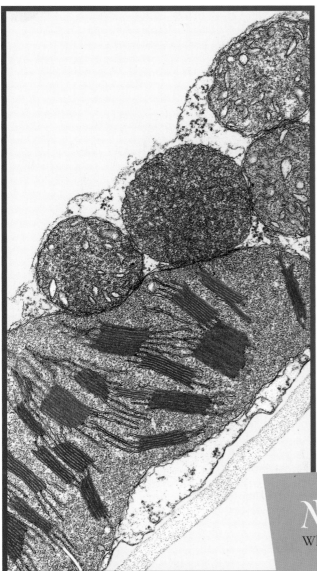

This photograph of a cell was taken through a microscope. The round structures at the top are chloroplasts.

The trapped light energy fuels a process called **photosynthesis**. During photosynthesis, water and a gas called **carbon dioxide** combine to form a sugary food called **glucose.** The water needed for photosynthesis is collected from the ground by the plant's roots. The carbon dioxide comes from the air. It enters a plant through tiny holes in the leaves.

Now I Know!

What is a leaf's most important job?

It collects sunlight.

19

When a bee lands on a flower, dusty
grains of pollen stick to its head and body.

How Do Plants Grow?

Plants use the food they make during photosynthesis to live and grow. Many plants also use their food to make beautiful flowers.

Roses, daisies, and snapdragons are just some of the flowers that grow in the warmer months. When flowers bloom, bees, butterflies, and other insects come to sip their sugary **nectar.** Tiny bits of powder called **pollen** stick to the insects' bodies.

While feeding on a flower's nectar, this butterfly picks up tiny grains of pollen.

When the insects move to a new flower, the pollen falls off their bodies. Some of the pollen then moves deep inside the flower. The flower uses pollen to make fruit with seeds inside.

This radish seed is breaking open. You can see the root and shoot pushing out.

Many animals like to eat fruit. When a bird munches on a juicy raspberry and then flies away, it carries the raspberry's seeds to a new place. The seeds pass through the bird's **digestive system** and land on the ground.

If the soil is rich, moist, and warm, some of the seeds will break open. New plants will begin to grow. They get the energy they need to sprout from food stored in the seed.

First a tiny root grows down into the ground. Then a shoot pushes up, breaking through the soil. As soon as the

It only takes a few days for a bean seed to grow into an adult plant.

Plants are everywhere, in all shapes and sizes. They are an important part of our world.

shoot appears, it begins to make leaves. Then the little plant can make food to fuel the rest of its growth.

Now I Know!

What is the sugary food insects are drawn to in flowers?

Nectar.

It may take weeks, months, or years, but one day the plant will make flowers and fruit of its own. It will also produce the seeds that will go on to form even more new plants.

 Activity

To learn more about how a plant grows, collect the following materials:

two plastic soda bottles
sand
potting soil
a packet of bush beans
two saucers
a notebook
pen
petroleum jelly

Part 1

1. Ask an adult to help you cut the top half off each soda bottle and punch several holes in its bottom.
2. Fill each bottle halfway with sand. Add 4 inches (10 centimeters) of soil to one bottle and 2 inches (5 centimeters) of soil to the other.
3. Plant four bush beans in each container, spacing them evenly along the edge of each bottle. Then place each

bottle on a saucer. Keep the soil moist, but do not soak it.

4. Observe the plants every day, and keep track of any changes you see in a notebook. How long does it take for the seeds to sprout? Do you see shoots or roots first? How long does it take for the shoot to break through the soil? Do you see any differences between the roots in the two bottles?

Part 2

1. Place one of the soda bottles in a dark place. Put the other one near a sunny window. What changes do you see after a week?

2. Move both bottles to the place where the plants grow best.

3. Spread petroleum jelly all over one leaf on a healthy plant. This will block air from entering tiny holes on the surface of the leaf. What changes do you see after a week? What do you think would happen if you covered all the leaves on a plant with petroleum jelly?

4. Stop watering the plants in one bottle. What changes do you see after a week? Name three things plants need to grow.

 Glossary

absorb—To soak up or take in.

carbon dioxide—An invisible gas in the air that is needed for photosynthesis.

cell—The basic building block of all living things.

chlorophyll—A green material found in plants that absorbs energy from the sun.

chloroplast—The organelle inside a plant cell that contains chlorophyll.

digestive system—The parts of an animal's body that work together to break down food.

energy—Something that provides living things with the power to carry out body processes.

glucose—The sugar made during photosynthesis.

habitat—The place where a plant or animal lives.

mineral—A material found in the ground that helps plants grow.

nectar—A sugary liquid many flowers make to attract insects and other animals, so they will spread the plant's pollen.

organelle—A compartment inside a cell.

oxygen—An invisible gas in the air. Animals need it to release energy from food.

photosynthesis—The process by which plants make food.

pollen—Powdery grains that must be sent to the female part of a flower or cone for seeds to be made.

species—A group of similar creatures that can mate and produce healthy young.

✿ Find Out More ✿

BOOKS

Burnie, David. *Plant*. New York: Dorling Kindersley, 2004.

Charman, Andrew. *I Wonder Why Trees Have Leaves: And Other Questions about Plants*. New York: Kingfisher, 1997.

Dorros, Arthur. *A Tree Is Growing*. New York: Scholastic, 1997.

Hewitt, Sally. *Plants and Flowers*. New York: Children's Press, 1998.

Stewart, Melissa. *A Parade of Plants*. Minneapolis: Compass Point Books, 2004.

WEB SITES

Environmental Kids Club
http://www.epa.gov/kids/
Learn to explore and protect the natural areas near your home.

KinderGarden
http://aggie-horticulture.tamu.edu/kindergarden/kinder.htm
For an introduction to the many ways children can interact with plants and the outdoors.

 Index

Page numbers for illustrations are in **boldface.**